Launch Pad:
Entrepreneur Workbook for Teens

TeenBizNetwork.com

Mary L Grothe

ISBN-13: 978-1511406253 ISBN-10: 1511406259

DEDICATION

This workbook is dedicated the hundreds of kids and teens I've had the privilege to serve and teach the concepts of business, money, and entrepreneurship. Empowering our young generation to become self-sustainable and successful before they graduate school is the most rewarding career and passion. Thank you for allowing me to be your teacher.

CONTENTS

INTRODUCTION

So you want to be an entrepreneur? What brought you to this point? Whatever it is, don't forget it. Hang on to that desire and passion, because being an entrepreneur is hard. It's risky. It's tiring. And at times it can drain you and push you to limits you didn't know existed. But it's all worth it. Owning a business, solving a problem, satisfying your customer, creating jobs, becoming self-sustainable are all results of becoming a good entrepreneur. Be prepared to fail. Be prepared to make mistakes. And be prepared to experience a life without limits, with uncapped success, and uncapped earning potential.

As a teenager, you might be worried that starting a business and running it will be harder for you than an adult. Trust me. It won't. The world is starving for change makers, thought leaders, innovators, inventors, and risk takers like you. Follow this workbook and learn how to turn your passion into a purpose, create an opportunity, and become an entrepreneur.

1 FRAMEWORK

Topics covered: Passion, mission, vision, framework, & company objective... what problem or challenge are you solving with your business?

Vocabulary words:

1) Entrepreneur – a person who creates and manages a business or organization which usually involves assuming a significant amount of risk.

2) Mission – the goal or purpose of the business or organization

3) Vision – anticipated future standing or results of the business or organization

4) Revenue – gross earnings of your business or organization

5) Capital – investment or money required to start the business or organization

The first exercise is to write out your business concept and ask yourself if you are in love with your business concept. But what does being in love with your business actually mean?

You need to determine if you are passionate about your business idea. People who turn their passion into their business model succeed at higher rates! In order to determine how passionate you can be about your business, first create your criteria of what would make you happy in your business. Perhaps break the criteria into categories for simplicity; type of customer, revenue, resources required for producing product, estimated amount of your involvement, need for employees/additional personnel resources, and/or capital needed to start the business.

Example Business Concept: Lawn Care Service

Customer	My Time	Capital	Revenue
Next Door Neighbor	Less than 10 hours per week	Don't need more than $100 to start	Can easily make $200+ per month
Has money to spend	Still have time to be a teenager	Can use customer's existing lawn equipment	Have at least 80% profit margins
Interested in outsourcing lawn care	Work mostly afternoons after school or weekends		20% revenue covers overhead

Example Business Concept: Cupcake Business

Customer	My Time	Capital	Revenue
Residential radius of 15 miles from my house for easy delivery	Less than 25 hours per week	Don't need more than $250 to start	Can easily make $200+ per month
Loves cupcakes	Still have time to be a teenager	Can start out of house	Have at least 50% profit margins
Will pay $3-$4 for a gourmet cupcake	Can bake the mornings orders before school	Bake to order, decrease food spoil/loss	

Write Out Your Business Concept:

_____

_____

_____

_____

Fill in your chart below:

Customer	My Time	Capital	Revenue

When you decide to become an entrepreneur, you have to be honest with yourself and try to identify the factors that could get in the way of your success. List out below three tough challenges that could get in the way! Perhaps you play a team sport that has a demanding schedule, perhaps you travel with your speech and debate team, or maybe your family goes skiing every weekend... what will get in the way of your success? Maybe it has to do with your personality. Are you a procrastinator? Do you get distracted easily? Are you a perfectionist? What about resources? Do you live in an area that's hard to get around in? Do you drive? What will limit you?

3 Tough Challenges That Could Get In the Way of You Being Successful:

1) _____

_____

_____

2) _____

_____

_____

3) _____

_____

_____

Let's start building out your concept!

Below, describe your mission and vision. The mission is about why you and your company are doing what you are doing. It is about how you affect your audience, market, the economy, the planet, and so on. Make it relevant and heartfelt. Your mission is the start to your marketing messaging and can be used in a variety of ways to create and support your brand. Your vision is just that; your vision. Where do you see your company 2, 3, or 20 years from now? Are you an industry leader? Will you solve an economic crisis or social issue? Tell your audience and competitors in your vision statement who they can expect your company to be. Make it a short, one sentence vision.

Mission:

_____

_____

_____

_____

_____

_____

Vision:

_____

_____

_____

_____

Now that your mission and vision are complete, start to write your company objective. Write a paragraph, like an introduction to your audience, on the company. Include information such as: when/where/why your company was founded and by who, the market need and market opportunity for what you do, and your differentiating factors. Now, you may not know your competition or the market need very well yet, but this is a good place to start.

Company Objective:

_____

_____

_____

_____

_____

_____

_____

_____

Now, start to think of what you will name your company. Be creative! But make sure your audience will understand the name. You want the company name to be easy to spell, briefly describe or at least indicate what you do, but be catchy, creative, and memorable. Try to avoid using your name or initials unless you can find a way to incorporate them while following the guideline's above.

Company Name

1) _____

2) _____

3) _____

2 MARKETING

Topics covered: Marketing, branding, the 4 P's, and competitive overview... how will your product or service compete in the marketplace?

Vocabulary words:

1) Marketing – the process and strategy of educating buyers about your product or service

2) Branding – the process and strategy of creating a distinguished, memorable look and feel to your product or service that is easily recognizable and remembered by your audience

3) The 4 P's

      a. Product – the product or service you are selling
      b. Price – the fee you charge for the product or service
      c. Place – where you sell or distribute your product or service
      d. Promotion – how you market, sell, and promote your product or service

4) Target audience – the audience that is most likely to buy from you, the group of people you tailor all your marketing messaging to, per their characteristics and desires

Small business owners say they are unique. When asked with whom they compete, they often say, "No one really does what I do. I mean, several business do {*insert your business idea here*}, but I do it better, I'm more experienced, and I have better technology and customer service". Trust me; there are lots of people out there doing what you are doing in your target audiences' eye. Your target audience is the group of people most likely to buy from you. They are not the expert on what you do! To them, you may look the same as the next guy. Don't say you're unique. We are all unique. Use compelling marketing messaging to explain your differentiating factors to your target audience.

Start conducting your market research now!

List out below what you find when you start researching your business idea on the internet. Use this area to simply write down some notes. How many other businesses have that business name? How many other businesses do what you do or sell what you sell? Who will be your competition? How are they marketing themselves? Premium brand? Cheap brand? Are they local? National? Start thinking about how you will differentiate yourself.

_____

_____

_____

_____

_____

_____

Market Analysis Summary

1) **Target Market Summary:** Start to narrow down your audience. Start by segmenting a group of people most likely to buy from you. Think about who your product or service would appeal to or help the most. Write down specifics about their geographic location, demographics, and lifestyle characteristics.

   Geographic:_____

   _____

   Demographic:_____

   _____

Lifestyle:_____

_____

2) **Market Trends**: Based on the market research you conducted on the Internet, list out the trends you're seeing regarding your specific idea. How many similar businesses are near yours? What is the predicted sales forecast for the industry your product/service fits in? What's hot right now? What's not hot?

_____

_____

_____

_____

_____

3) **Market Growth**: This is where you need to think about market potential. Is the industry you're in going to grow? Is it on the decline? What does your market research show about the potential your product/service has to grow over the next 5-10 years?

_____

_____

_____

4) **Market Needs**: Perhaps your product or service serves a specific market need. Explain how your product/service solves a problem in society, the economy, in a specific geographic location, or for a specific demographic.

_____

_____

_____

Marketing strategy is very important. Without it, you might have the best product or service that ever existed... but no one would know about it, and you'd never sell it.

Marketing Mix – The marketing mix refers to the 4 P's: Product, Price, Place, and Promotion

1) **Product:** clearly define your product/service. You and your company may be <u>very</u> good at a lot of things, but do not scare your audience by coming out of the gate with 10 different products or services. Choose one or two! Once you build brand recognition and credibility, release more products/services.

_____

_____

_____

_____

_____

_____

2) **Price:** There are two ways to price your product. Base it on market price or cost of goods sold. Within market price, there are three ways to price it. Under market (means you are the Wal-Mart, McDonald's, Dollar Store equivalent), at market price (means you are the Target, Macy's, Chili's equivalent) or at above market price, or premium price (like Whole Foods, Luis Vuitton, or Del Frisco's Steakhouse). Each has its benefits. Choose wisely. Pricing your product/service by cost of goods sold means you've calculated how much money it costs you (your company) to make/offer your product/service and you base the price on your cost + profit you'd like to make. Discuss your pricing method below.

_____

_____

_____

_____

_____

3) **Place:** Place refers to where you are going to sell/offer your product or service. Define this. Many small business owners have a dream of going national or global within months. For few, it is feasible. Ask yourself. Is it feasible for you? My recommendation is start within a 15 mile radius of your home/office if you're delivering a physical product performing a "hands-on" service. This will be helpful when you develop your promotion methods; especially if you can promote your business through networking channels, associations, and community. Start local, build your brand first. Grow when you're ready. Big dreams are good, but so is reality! Write out where you will sell your product/service below.

_____

_____

_____

_____

4) **Promotion**: Types of promotion methods are practically endless in today's marketing trends. Below is a short list to consider.

    1) Sales and Strategic Relationships (partnerships)

    2) Chambers/Associations

3) Launch Party/Event Hosting

4) Social Media

    a. Facebook

    b. Google

    c. Twitter

    d. Linked In

    e. You Tube

    f. Instagram

5) Traditional Methods

    a. Radio

    b. TV

    c. Magazine

    d. Print Ads

    e. Sponsorships

Develop a strategy for each of the promotional methods that pertain to your business. Remember, a certain method may not work for one market, but may work extremely well for another. Be detailed in this area and use this next page of space to write out a detailed promotion plan using at least three of the methods listed above.

_____

_____

_____

_____

_____

_____

_____

_____

_____

_____

_____

_____

_____

_____

_____

_____

_____

_____

_____

_____

Main Competitors: Go back to your market research and list the main competitors you found below.

_____

_____

_____

In an effort to really understand your competitive advantage, you must create an understanding of your competitive landscape. When you start the competitive landscape, you need to build a competitive analysis table. An example of this table is shown next. Please note this is simply a short example. Professional competitive analysis tables contain much more data and can be pages in length.

Competitor	Pricing	Services/Product	Location	Customer Reviews
AJ's Lawn Care	$15/hr flat	Mowing, raking, trimming, weeds	Denver, CO	No reviews, no web presence
Bart's Mowing	$20 per mow	Mowing	Aurora, CO	67% satisfaction rating on Google reviews
Carl's Landscaping	$50-$500 range per service	Complete landscaping designs + basic lawn care maintenance	25 Locations in CO	Over 90% satisfaction, boasted about on their website

Your competitive analysis table:

Company	Pricing	Services/Product	Location	Other

Competitive Analysis Notes: Use this space for more notes on your competitive research!

_____

_____

_____

_____

_____

_____

_____

Once you have created your competitive analysis table, start listing out the main differentiating factors you see. Easy categories to start with are specific product or services offered, pricing, and customer service. It's important that you go through these steps to REALLY know your business inside and out!

Differentiating Factors:

1) _____

_____

_____

2) _____

_____

_____

3) _____

_____

_____

4) _____

_____

_____

3 FINANCIAL

Topics covered: Revenue streams, financial framework, profit/loss, expenses, basic budgeting... how will your business be profitable?

Vocabulary words:

1) Revenue – gross earnings of your business or organization

2) Expenses – total costs to run the business organization

3) Profit – all money left over from your revenue once your expenses are paid

4) Pro Forma – indicates hypothetical financial figures based on business operation assumptions

There are important revenue streams in business. You need to find a way to make money through as many of them as you can. The table below names, defines, and illustrates each type.

Example:

Revenue Stream	Payment Terms	Example
Immediate	Paid Immediately	Cupcakes sold by the single, half dozen, or dozen. They are ordered and paid for at the same time, allowing your organization to recoup costs quickly.
Long-Term	Paid Consistently Over a Period of Time	Create a "cupcake of the month" program where each loyal customer receives a dozen of your new flavor of the month! Automatically charge their credit card when the cupcakes are made and delivered. Ask for a 3-6 month commitment and get an agreement & terms signed. This long-term revenue helps you predict cash flow. Offer a discount for singing up!
Residual	Paid monthly over a period of 12+ months	Create a monthly subscription to a private online blog where you send out a recipe each months and a how-to baking video! Charge $2.99 per person and require 12 months minimum!

Now it's time to create your chart! Get creative!

Revenue Stream	Payment Terms	Description
Immediate		
Long Term		
Residual		

Some entrepreneurs struggle to find three ways they can ask a customer for money. While you are completing this exercise, understand that your buyer does <u>not</u> have to know how you make money. Find ways to create additional revenue streams using verticals, revenue shares, and the internet.

Here is an example. As entrepreneurs, we all need a website. Additionally, we all sell to a target market. There are hundreds of businesses also selling into that same target market. Find a non-competing industry that is selling into your target market and offer paid advertising on your website. These strategically placed partners are viewed as a value-add to your audience, but they are making you money! Set up these advertisers on auto-billed recurring monthly billing. For your lawn care business, maybe you could sell website advertising to a company that offers window installation, roofing services, in-home health care, etc. All of these companies advertise to your same target audience, but they do not compete with you! Sell them a small web ad on your website for $25 per month. Not much money to them, but if you get 10 of those advertisers, that's $250 per month, residual revenue if you ask for a 12 month contract!

Accepting payment is always a sticky situation. Asking for money is not easy for many of us. Create client agreements that are clear, concise, and ensure <u>every</u> customer signs one! Many times, we do business with our friends and family. They are no exception! In fact, friends and family are the worst offenders when it comes to not paying invoices. Contracts and agreements can be set up in a variety of ways, but be sure the following is included:

1) Clearly written section on how fees are calculated

2) Clearly written section on when payment is due

3) Clearly written section on how payment can be made

4) Clearly written section on scope of services

5) Clearly written section on terms of agreement

6) Clearly written section on terms of past due payments

The recurring theme here is obviously "clearly written". Many agreements and contracts are too wordy and leave room for different interpretations. Make sure both parties understand the agreement in its entirety. Many times you'll find yourself in a position to have to check on payment status as many small business owners do business with other small business owners. Many small business owners have cash flow issues. Do not be a victim of accounts receivable! Depending on the scope of work, try asking for a 50% deposit or a retainer for services. Lastly, under no circumstance should you give out your services for free. Discounts? Maybe. Protect your time! Show your value from the first day you do business.

PRO FORMA

The first step to creating a Pro Forma is to complete your financial assumptions. Let's start by selecting your key performance indicators (KPIs). For a business, KPIs can be average revenue per sale, average cost of goods sold, profit margins, average hourly calculated rate per service, cost per lead source (cost of acquiring a customer per promotion or sales method), and attrition rate (loss rate of customers). All these KPIs are examples; you need to find four to five KPIs that when used consistently, provide accurate data that helps you manage your business and make business decisions.

To make this clear, here is an example. See the following table. This is the start to building our assumptions for the financial data.

KPI Description	Target Amount
Average Revenue per Sale	$36/dozen cupcakes
Average Cost of Goods Sold	$18/dozen cupcakes
Profit Margin Target	50%

KPI Description	Target

When creating your pro forma, you will want to make additional financial assumptions such as, I can only work 10 hours per week. I can only mow 12 lawns in 10 hours. I charge $20 per mow, therefore unless I hire more employees or expand the amount of time I work per week, I can only make $240 in gross revenue per week from that one revenue stream. For the cupcake business, you may only be able to bake so many cupcakes before school. Perhaps you will max out on orders… you should think about the financial assumptions and when growth/expansion will need to take place in your business. Perhaps you can hire your friend, sibling, or parent to help you in your business. Find a way to maximize your opportunity with low overhead. Whatever your financial assumptions are, write them down here. Keeping these assumptions handy will help when you create the pro forma and it will also help when others (like mentors/business investors).

Financial Assumptions:

1)

2)

3)

4)

5)

6)

7)

Next is a sample pro forma. This is a service business that has one employee. You can see that revenue and expenses grow over time as the company is expanding. Typically, we forget about little line items and they sneak up on us. Write out every possible revenue and expense you can think of for your business in the blank chart following this example.

EXAMPLE PRO FORMA:

REVENUE	Jun-15	Jul-15	Aug-15	Sep-15	Oct-15
Teaching Revenue	4500	5000	5500	6500	7000
Consulting Revenue	2500	3000	3500	4000	4500
Product Revenue	2000	2500	3000	3500	4000
Membership Revenue	0	0	200	300	500
TOTAL	**9000**	**10500**	**12200**	**14300**	**16000**

EXPENSES					
Employee #1 Payroll	1500	2000	2500	2500	3000
Accountant/Payroll Fees	700	700	700	700	700
Networking	250	250	250	250	250
Advertising	775	775	1000	1600	2000
Phone/Internet	190	190	190	190	190
Website	0	2000	1500	500	500
Social Media	170	500	750	1000	1000
Mobile Apps	2000	50	50	50	50
Owner Salary	1000	2000	2500	5000	5000
TOTAL	**6585**	**8465**	**9440**	**11790**	**12690**
PROFIT	2415	2035	2760	2510	3310
Current Cash	0	2415	4450	7210	9720
Revenue	9000	10500	12200	14300	16000
Payroll	2500	4000	5000	7500	8000
Expenses	4085	4465	4440	4290	4690
Balance	$2415	$4450	$7210	$9720	$13,030

Your chart:

Month ->					
Revenue 1					
Revenue 2					
Revenue 3					
TOTAL REVENUE					

Expense 1					
Expense 2					
Expense 3					
Expense 4					
Expense 5					
Expense 6					
Expense 7					
Expense 8					
Expense 9					
TOTAL EXPENSES					
Profit					
Current Cash					
Revenue					
Payroll					
Expenses					
Balance					

4 SALES

Topics covered: Sales strategy, customer acquisition strategy… how will you earn business and gain new customers?

Vocabulary words:

  1) Sales – the process and strategy of acquiring customers

  2) Acquisition/Acquiring – the act of winning a new customer and earning their business

This next section allows you to understand not what you sell, but what your clients and/or audience wants to buy from you. Dale Carnegie has a fantastic sales exercise in the "How to Sell Like a Pro" class. The instructor holds up an everyday object and asks the students to shout out what they're really buying when they buy that object. Below are some examples.

Camera = Memories

Chocolate = Satisfaction

Hole Puncher = Holes

How does this relate to your business? Here are some examples:

Personal Trainer = Confidence, Self-Esteem

Real Estate = A Lifelong Dream

Cupcakes = Sweet satisfaction

Lawn Mowing = Cut Grass

Motivational Speaker = Higher Productivity from Employees

Car = Ability to get to Work & School

Now list out what you sell or do, and what your target actually buys:

1) _____ = _____

2) _____ = _____

3) _____ = _____

Completing a SWOTT analysis table helps you understand exactly how you're different, why your customers/audience would want to buy from you, your areas for improvement, market opportunities, potential threats to your business, and trends (buying behavior, economy, technology) that will impact your business. SWOTT stands for:

S – Strengths

W – Weaknesses

O – Opportunities

T – Threats

T – Trends

	Strengths	Weaknesses	Opportunities	Threats	Trends
You					
Product/Service					
Company					

The next step in understanding how to communicate your differentiating factors is first understanding how your target audience needs to be spoken to in order to be heard. In the previous section, you identified your target audience. Use the demographic and psychographic factors to understand how they need to be spoken to as you learn more about developing your messaging.

Messaging:

Look at all the products/services you buy, personally in your life right now. Why did you buy them? How did that company speak to you through their messaging? What did they say or how did they say it? Did they use cute characters, animation, bright colors, sad stories, scary scenarios? A good way to start crafting your messaging is to look at your competitors. Do not recreate the wheel. Find out who your top three competitors are and analyze their messaging across all their channels. Pay attention for these:

1) Channel or method of communication (radio, TV, print, a specific website, social media site)

2) Tone of message (fear, happiness, excitement, sadness)

3) Length of message (15/30 second ad, full print article)

4) Frequency of message (every commercial break, printed in every publication, social media blast weekly)

5) Diversity of channels (how many places/channels do you hear or see this company?)

6) Call to action (what do they ask their audience to do? Register for an event, visit a website, order online, download something, go to their store, test drive a car?)

Make sure you test your messaging with your target audience. Trust me, you know <u>way</u> too much about what you do! And NO ONE CARES. They only care about what is in it for them! Speak to them!

Use the next page to begin writing your messaging. It's alright to make mistakes. Try narrowing down to one message, but change the length and call to action so you have several options for messaging across different channels/methods, but with consistency.

Messaging examples:

_____

_____

_____

_____

_____

_____

More:

_____

_____

_____

_____

_____

_____

Keep Practicing:

_____

_____

_____

_____

_____

_____

10 Second Pitch:

_____

_____

_____

_____

_____

30 Second Pitch:

_____

_____

_____

_____

_____

_____

_____

Full Pitch:

_____

_____

_____

_____

_____

_____

_____

_____

5 LAUNCH

Topics covered: Product/service launch strategy: includes all the keys to success, final version of the sales, marketing, finance, and exit strategy and overall answer to: what is your go to market strategy?

Vocabulary words:

1) Sourcing – the distribution channels you can use to sell your product/service

As you complete this final section of the workbook, complete your answers with words that could be reused in your marketing, website content, meetings with business mentors, or potential investors. This is a good time to ensure you double check your work and feel confident about your brand! Additionally, you can use these words in your presentation for the business plan competition, if the program or school implementing this curriculum has included the business plan competition.

Keys to Success - The keys to success are two-three main points that sum up what you, your company, and your product/service must do or deliver to ensure your company's success.

_____

_____

_____

_____

_____

Start-up Summary - The start-up summary describes what the company needs financially, operationally, and logistically to startup. You must be able to clearly articulate what your needs are if you are presenting this business to an investor or as part of the competition.

_____

_____

_____

_____

_____

_____

_____

_____

Product and Services Description – This section gives you the opportunity to list, in detail, all your products and services. List every revenue stream as well.

_____

_____

_____

_____

_____

_____

_____

_____

Sales Literature – Sales literature is important because it gives your potential customer an idea of your brand and what you offer. You need to list out all the types of sales literature you will create for your business. Describe the marketing brochures, slicks, business cards, and collateral you will use and how it will be created. For the lawn care business example, you could create a one page flyer for your neighbors and residents in a 2 mile radius. You could design the flyer to have all your services and fees listed out along with your contact information. Don't forget a catchy tagline and an eye-catching photo. For the business plan competition, you should have samples prepared.

_____

_____

_____

_____

_____

Sourcing – Sourcing describes the distribution channels of your product/service. For some industries, this is a difficult section to complete because multiple channels do not exist. Write out a short paragraph that explains through what or whom your product/service can be distributed or sold if more than one exists. For example, if you have a cupcake business, perhaps you can bake 5 dozen cupcakes every morning and take them to a local coffee shop who buys them from you for $2.50 per cupcake and they sell them for $3.50 per piece. They keep the $1 per cupcake, and you still make $1 per cupcake (as long as you keep your expenses at $1.50 per cupcake).

_____

_____

_____

_____

_____

_____

_____

Technology –Use this section to create a visual outline of your technology needs for your business! Most businesses are now building mobile apps, mobile websites, and a standard website as part of their technology suite. Include high-level information on all these. What will your domain name be? Where will you buy it? Where will it be hosted? Which app builder will you choose for the mobile app? Will you use an RSS Feed, social media feed? Will you need an e-commerce plug-in so you can sell your product over the internet?

_____

_____

_____

_____

_____

_____

_____

Future Products – This is the perfect section to illustrate your dream! Use this space to describe in a couple of paragraphs the potential of where this company can go! Think about adding more revenue streams, enhancing the current product, or aligning with strategic partners to create the best must-have product or service. A good example of a strategic alliance is when Hershey's teamed up with Graham Crackers and Marshmallows to make S'mores!

_____

_____

_____

_____

_____

_____

_____

_____

Website Marketing Strategy – The website marketing strategy outlines every way you plan on using your website to market your business or run your business. Be sure to discuss SEO & PPC strategies here and any other web marketing techniques you will be incorporating. If you are a business that requires high website traffic to be successful, this section really needs to be thought out and contain details regarding how you will drive traffic! Do not confuse this with social media marketing; although social media does help drive traffic to your website.

_____

_____

_____

_____

_____

_____

_____

Sales Strategy - Your sales strategy should be a multi-step process. This is a good time to start thinking about what type of sales personnel you will need in the future as you grow, how they will represent you in the marketplace, and through what channels (telemarketing, networking, and/or outside sales) they will sell. To start, you may be the only person selling your product. Down the road, perhaps a family member or friend can join forces with you and help promote your business using the promotion methods we discussed earlier.

_____

_____

_____

_____

_____

_____

Sales Forecast – You should forecast at least one year of sales projections based on the data in the pro forma. Write out a short paragraph that explains where the revenue is coming from (how much revenue from each of the revenue sources we discussed), what causes increases or decreases, and what other revenue streams might come into play over time (this info comes from your "future products" section previously completed).

_____

_____

_____

Year 1 Sales Example:

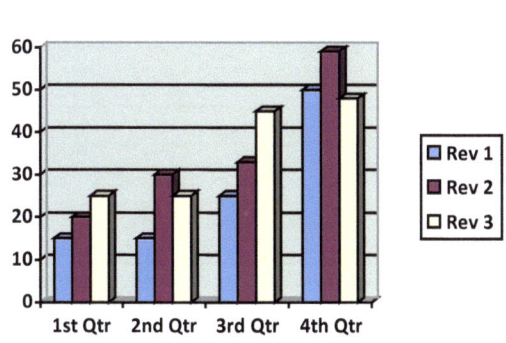

Strategic Alliances – Strategic alliances are super important. Here you can outlines several ways you can grow your company. Think about the s'mores example again! Think big picture here. With whom could you align down the road that could help make your company stronger, bigger, and better by forming small partnerships or joining a trifecta? List all those options here!

_____

_____

_____

_____

Value Proposition – Your value proposition will carry you as you begin marketing and selling your product/service. Without this, you really do not have a business. Trust me, we have seen it. You may build a great business, but if you cannot tell your audience why they benefit from using you or buying your product, you have little to no sales. Create a paragraph here that tells your "why" and "what's in it for them" in just 2-3 short sentences! You will use this value prop over and over in your marketing messaging and sales!

_____

_____

_____

_____

_____

_____

Management Summary – The management summary is a short paragraph that lists the members on your team and their involvement with the company. To start, this may just be you… but as it grows overtime, be sure you document everyone's responsibilities!

_____

_____

_____

_____

Management Team – People will often ask about the credibility of you and your management team members. The management team summary allows you to include a full professional biography on everyone who is part of the management team. Investors and strategic partners may like to see who is running and behind your business. Additionally, you will be asked down the road to provide bios of your team. It is helpful to have these created on the front end so you can do some cutting and pasting when needed. You can write down some notes here, but just use this section as a reminder to get your bios stored in your documents folder on your computer.

_____

_____

_____

_____

_____

_____

_____

Break-Even Analysis – Every investor, strategic partner, and employee should want to know when the company plans on reaching critical mass, or when it breaks even. This is when the company can actually turn a profit. Plus, it is just really good for you to know when that date is so you have a goal to work towards and can celebrate it when you achieve it! If your business requires little to no capital to start and has low monthly expenses, you may break even in your first month! But if you have to spend lots of money on equipment, materials, technology, marketing, or branding, you may take a few months to break even. Just take the time to write about it here! The data will be in your Pro Forma.

_____

_____

_____

Exit Strategy – Every business owner must begin with the end in mind! You should know from the beginning if this is a three year, five year, ten year, or pass-down-to-family, type of business. Most companies now sell within three to five years; especially in the technology industry. Most services-based companies still last about five to ten years. Very rarely are businesses being built that are planning on being passed down through the family; generation after generation. The exit strategy should be very detailed. It should explain who the main players are in the company at the management team level, who plans on working in what role, who plans on stepping aside after a certain amount of time, what the succession plan is, who a potential buyer of the company would be, in what time frame would the company start looking for buyers (what milestones need to be hit, as an example), and/or go IPO. These are several examples of the questions you should ask yourself. A company can take two to three years to sell. Be sure you discuss this strategy with other management team members.

_____

_____

_____

_____

_____

_____

Steps to officially LAUNCHING your business!

- ☐ Find a committed business mentor to help you through the launch process.

- ☐ Decide on final business name.

- ☐ Buy the domain name.

- ☐ Host the domain name.

- ☐ Get some professional looking photos done of you that you can use for marketing.

- ☐ Choose your color scheme (pick 2-3 colors that represent your brand and ONLY use them from here on out).

- ☐ Choose your font style that you will use for your business! Super important to be consistent with the font that you choose.

- ☐ Create a logo or hire someone to create one for you!

- ☐ Start building your website. You can build it very easily through some of the web builder click and drop/drag programs or you can hire someone.

- ☐ Use your marketing messaging, mission, vision, and company objectives as a start for content on your website.

- ☐ Set up your ecommerce if applicable (this can take a few days for your bank account to be verified) and link it to your website.

- ☐ Create your business LinkedIn, Facebook, & Twitter page and any other social media sites you have decided to use per the promotions section of this workbook.

- ☐ Make business cards and get them printed.

- ☐ Start telling people about your business! Attend networking/chamber events, attend local entrepreneur MeetUp groups, use social media and the other promotion methods.

- ☐ Track your daily to-do's and stay organized. Be sure to track all your expenses and revenue. Make sure you follow through on all your customer commitments!

- ☐ Create systems and processes around your work week. Create a time management calendar and follow simple processes to ensure every task is completed. Change what doesn't work and replicate what does.

- ☐ Always ask for help when you get stuck or overwhelmed.

- ☐ Don't quit when the going gets tough... ask for help!

- ☐ Be proud of yourself, but stay humble and be willing to coach and help others.

- ☐ Take a leadership role amongst your friends and prove to them that teens can create a successful and self-sustainable life before they graduate High School!

☐ Take advantage of media interviews and opportunities in the spotlight to help promote the #TeenBizNetwork and #TeenEntrepreneurs movement.

☐ Use the #TeenBizNetwork hashtag when you want us to know how you are doing... and when you are ready, reach out to us so we can FEATURE YOUR BUSINESS!!!

Until then, remember this... the successful entrepreneurial equation is to turn your passion into a purpose that creates opportunity for others; which ultimately creates opportunity for you.

Stay strong and happy business building!

ABOUT THE AUTHOR

Mary Grothe is a 7 year business strategist who accomplished a 2-peat #1 sales title for Fortune 1000 company Paychex, Inc., led the sales and marketing division for a Denver-based start-up while quadrupling their revenue in less than a year, ran her business consulting practice for 3 years, published three books, and created a TV & Radio show teaching the youth about business, money, and entrepreneurship... all before she turned 30. Mary has now returned to Paychex, focusing on engaging with HR and CxO level professionals within midsize companies in Downtown Denver, CO, to lead conversations about the employee life cycle and create strategies to align the business and HR/employee initiatives of the organization.

Mary also proudly serves as Vice President of the Board of Directors for new entrepreneurial charter school, Launch High School, in Colorado Springs, CO, and plans to invest time to grow the concept nationally.

Lastly, her latest book, Launch Pad: Entrepreneur Workbook for Teens, is now being implemented in several school districts and youth programs across the nation as an opt-in after-school instructor taught curriculum. Please contact Mary if you're interested in implementing the 5-week course for your school or program. Learn more at http://teenbiznetwork.com.